Helen Marlais'
Succeeding at the Piano

A Method for Everyone

For the Student

Throughout this book you will do many different activities such as:

Writing:

After you write the answers, you can play them on the piano.

Rhythm:

Just as this boy and girl walk in rhythm together, you will feel the steady beat in every rhythm activity!

Time to Compose:

Your very own compositions can be just as important as the pieces you learn.

Ear Training:

Learn notes and patterns in music by using your ears carefully.

Follow the Leader:

Use your ears to hear *rhythmic* patterns.

Parrot Play:

Use your ears to hear *musical* patterns.

Production: Frank J. Hackinson
Production Coordinators: Joyce Loke and Satish Bhakta
Editors: Joyce Loke, Edwin McLean, Peggy Gallagher, and
   Nancy Bona-Baker
Art Direction: Andi Whitmer – in collaboration with Helen Marlais
Cover Illustration: ©2010 Susan Hellard/Arena
Interior Illustrations: ©2011 Teresa Robertson/Arena
Cover and Interior Illustration Concepts: Helen Marlais
Engraving: Tempo Music Press, Inc.
Printer: Tempo Music Press, Inc.

ISBN-13: 978-1-56939-938-5

THE
F·J·H
MUSIC
COMPANY
INC.
Frank J. Hackinson

Grade 2B - Table of Contents

UNIT 1

Pick the Lemons for Lemonade

(Review of Music Symbols and Terms from Grade 2A)

Draw a line from the musical symbol or term in each lemon to its correct definition on the ground below.

damper pedal   dotted quarter note   return to the   *diminuendo*
                                                    original tempo   or ———

         eighth notes   triad   *fermata*

key signature—   *ritardando*
all F's in the piece   first and second   (gradually slowing
are sharp   endings   down)

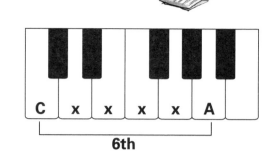

Learning 6ths

1. Find any C on the piano. Going higher skip 4 white keys and find A. This is a 6th!

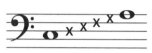

6th

On the staff, a 6th looks like this:

space to line,
4 skipped notes

line to space,
4 skipped notes

2.

Note Challenge No. 1:
Play Bass C. Go down a 4th, then go up a 3rd. Lastly, go down a 6th. What is the letter name of the key you land on? _____

Note Challenge No. 2:
Play Guide Note G. Go up a 5th. Go up a 6th. Lastly, go down a 3rd. What is the letter name of the key you land on? _____

3. Answer the following questions as fast as a lightening bolt. Time yourself by using a clock.

  • Draw an X on the nearest guide note to help you.

  • Write the interval and the letter name of the notes.

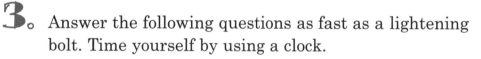

Ex.   6th up

A   F

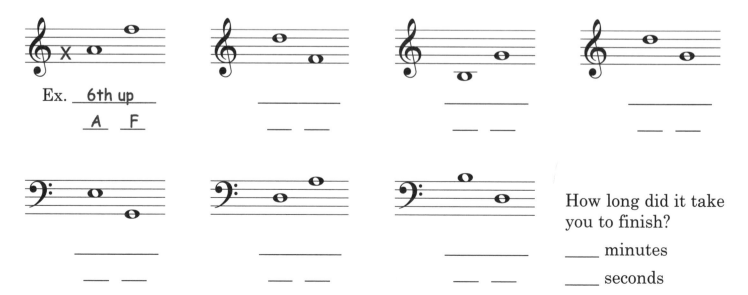

How long did it take you to finish?

____ minutes

____ seconds

FJH2068

Help Apollo the Dog

- Apollo is looking for doggy bones today.
- Write "M" for a melodic interval, and "H" for a harmonic interval.
- Draw an X on the nearest guide note.
- Then write the letter names.
- Find and play every 6th.

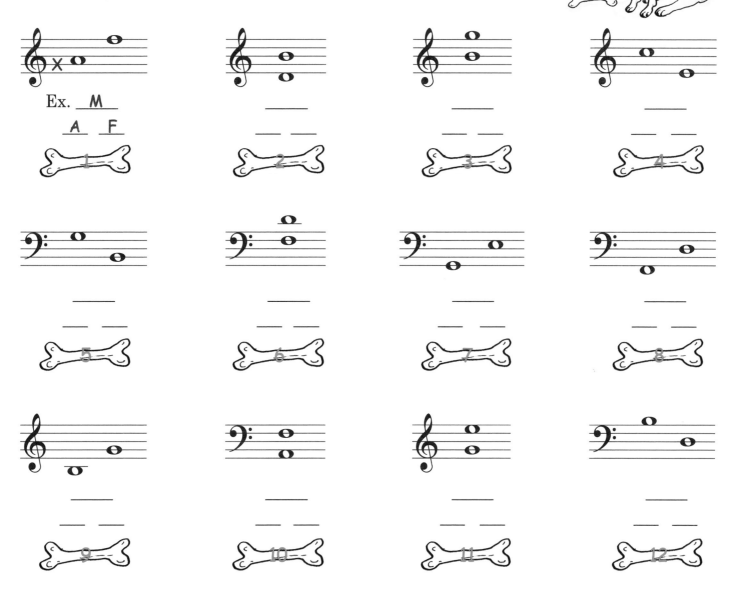

For teachers: (How many are correct? _____ /12)

Extra Credit

- Draw the following intervals from these guide notes.
- Then name the note you drew.

Melodic 6th up   Harmonic 6th up   Harmonic 6th up   Melodic 6th up

Parrot Play:

Parrots love to repeat what they hear!

- Your teacher will play *Hush, Little Baby.*
- Can you sing it together and sway to the beat?
- Listen to the intervals of a 6th. Sing this song to remember the 6th.

Key signature:
(sharp all _____)
you write

Hush, Little Baby
Traditional

Hush, lit-tle ba-by, don't say a word, Ma-ma's gon-na buy you a mock-ing-bird.

If that mock-ing-bird don't sing, Ma-ma's gon-na buy you a dia-mond ring.

☐ Check the box when you can play this song.

Ear Training:

- Let's review other intervals by singing these songs:

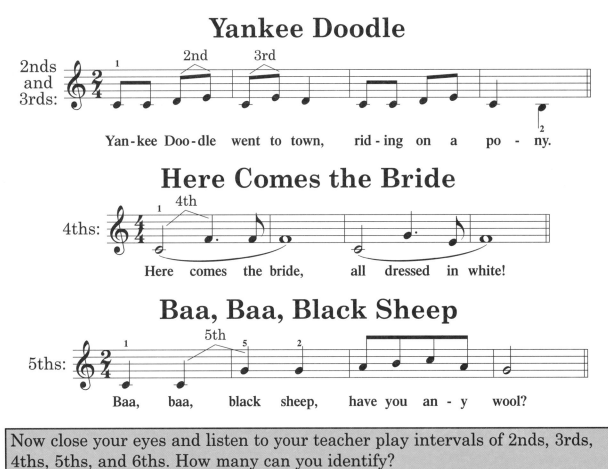

Yankee Doodle

2nds and 3rds:

Yan-kee Doo-dle went to town, rid-ing on a po-ny.

Here Comes the Bride

4ths:

Here comes the bride, all dressed in white!

Baa, Baa, Black Sheep

5ths:

Baa, baa, black sheep, have you an-y wool?

Now close your eyes and listen to your teacher play intervals of 2nds, 3rds, 4ths, 5ths, and 6ths. How many can you identify?

Fun with 6ths and Famous Melodies

- Find and circle the melodic 6ths in the melodies below.
- Then play the melodies. Keep in mind the key signature!

Little Tommy Tucker
Traditional

Lit - tle Tom-my Tuck - er, he sang for his sup - per.

Home on the Range
Traditional

Oh, give me a home where the buf - fa - lo roam.

Symphony No. 40
by W. A. Mozart

String Quartet
(Op. 76, No. 3)
by F. J. Haydn

Time to Compose:

- Make up your own piece using 6ths. Will it be in $\frac{2}{4}$, $\frac{3}{4}$ or $\frac{4}{4}$?
- Decide the tempo: *Adagio, Andante, Moderato, Allegretto,* or *Allegro*?
- Use ♩ ♪ and decide the form.   My title: _____

Fun with Finger Crossings

- Circle the **three** places in the music where you will make a finger crossing.
- Then play the piece.

I Love The Spring

Traditional

Moderato

R.H.

L.H.

mf

I love the Spring, when sleep - ing birds are wak - ened

in - to flight,_____ when joy and glad - ness seem to

spread, and days are so warm and so bright!_____

Parrot Play:

- Your teacher will play a pattern from each set below.
- Which pattern do you hear, a or b?
- Play the one you hear.
- Then circle it.

1a.

2a.

1b.

2b.

Follow the Leader:

- Listen to your teacher clap the rhythms on the right.
- Listen to the strong downbeats.
- Can you clap them back?

A Sea of 6ths

- Circle all of the harmonic 6ths.
- Write the letter names next to all of the notes.
- Then play them.

The C Major Scale

- A scale uses every letter of the musical alphabet in order.

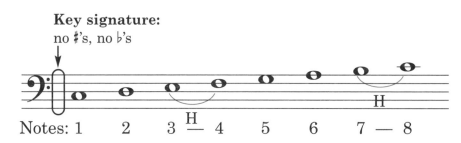

- A major scale **always** has a half step between notes 3-4 and 7-8. This is what makes it sound **major**.
- Notice the whole steps between the other notes.

- Each scale has a **key signature** to keep the major scale pattern of two half steps between notes 3 and 4, and 7 and 8.
- C Major does not need any ♯'s or ♭'s to keep the pattern.

Forgetful Freddie has forgotten the C Major Scale!

- Cross out the **two** incorrect notes in the scale below and correct them.
- Now mark the two half steps, going up and going down.
- Then play the scale *legato* while saying the correct fingering aloud.

Reviewing the Three Important Notes in the C Major Scale:

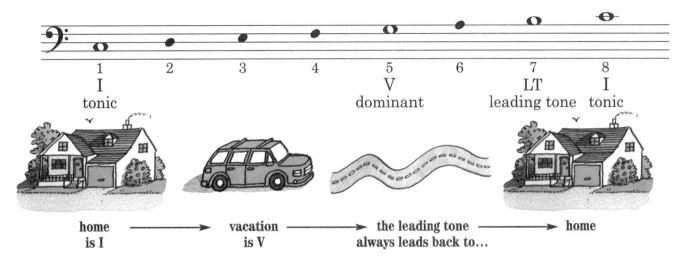

1	2	3	4	5	6	7	8
I				V		LT	I
tonic				dominant		leading tone	tonic

home → vacation → the leading tone → home
is I is V always leads back to...

- Write the correct notes on the staff. Then play them.

I	V	LT	I
tonic	dominant	leading tone	tonic

Ear Training:

Lightly Row

- Play the melody of this folk song.
- Then, by ear, play the I and V⁷ chords in the L.H.
- Write in the missing chords and play the entire piece.

mf Light - ly row,   light - ly row,   O'er the glass - y   waves we go!

(Write the missing chords . . .)

I   V⁷   I   V⁷

Smooth - ly glide,   smooth - ly glide,   on the si - lent   tide.

The Parts of the Piano

• Fill in the name of the notes to complete the story.

TH_   PI_NO   "_ _TION"   H_S   S_V_R_L

THOUS_N_   MOVIN_   P_RTS   TH_T   WORK

TO_ _TH_R.   SOME OF THEM ARE:

STRIN_ _ S,   H_M M_RS,   PINS,   P_ _ _ LS,

_ _ MP_RS,   K_YS,   _N_   TH_

SOUN_ _O_R_.

A MAN IN ITALY NAMED _RISTO_ORI*

INV_NT_ _ THE PIANO AROUND 1781.

(* Pronounced krees-toh-**FOHR**-ee)

   FJH2068

Ear Training:

- Your teacher will play a C Major scale first.
- Then your teacher will play a 2nd, 3rd, 4th, 5th, or 6th starting on C.
- Without looking at the piano, write the interval you hear.
  (Use the songs you learned on page 6 to help you!)

1. _____ 2. _____ 3. _____

4. _____ 5. _____ 6. _____

For teacher use: (To be played in any order.)

Time to Compose:

- Create a piece using I and V⁷ chords in the L.H., shown below.
- Write down your melody, using ♫, ♩, and ♩. ♪ rhythms in your R.H.
- When using the I chord, use mostly triad tones (1-3-5) in the melody, and when using the V⁷ chord, use mostly non-triad tones (2-4) in the melody.

Andante   Moderato
(choose your tempo)

_____
(your title)

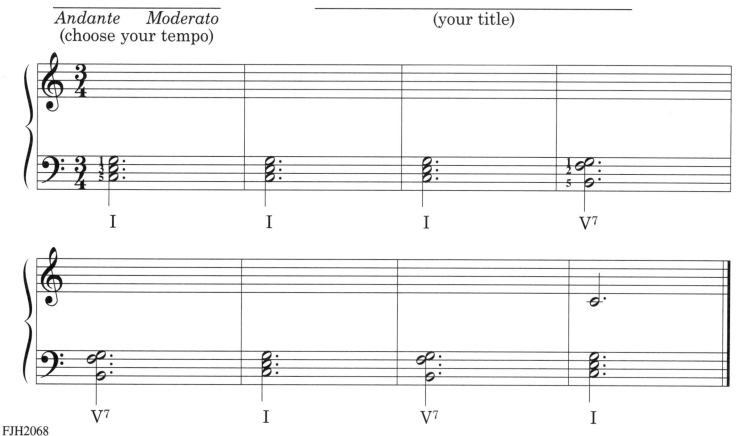

The G Major Scale

- In the G Major scale below, mark the two half steps between notes 3-4 and 7-8.
- Notice that the key of G Major needs one sharp (F♯) to keep the major pattern.

Key signature

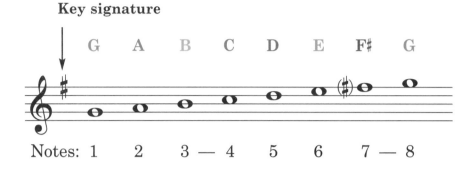

Notes: 1   2   3 — 4   5   6   7 — 8

- Trace the F♯'s in the key signature below.
- Then draw the key signature for G Major twice on your own.

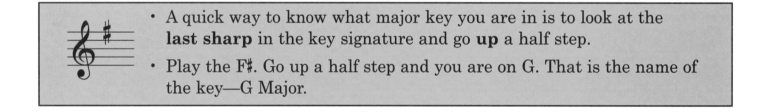

- A quick way to know what major key you are in is to look at the **last sharp** in the key signature and go **up** a half step.
- Play the F♯. Go up a half step and you are on G. That is the name of the key—G Major.

- Write a G Major scale in the Treble Clef, ascending and descending. Keep in mind to write the F♯ in front of the correct notes.

- In the Bass Clef below, draw the key signature after the clef sign.
- Then, write a G Major scale, ascending and descending.
- Add the fingering and play it.

- Draw the key signature for G Major.
- Then write the correct notes on the staff and play them.

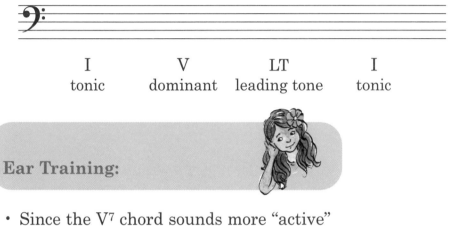

| I | V | LT | I |
| tonic | dominant | leading tone | tonic |

Ear Training:

- Since the V⁷ chord sounds more "active" than the tonic triad, *crescendo* to the measures that use V⁷ harmony.

The King of France

Traditional

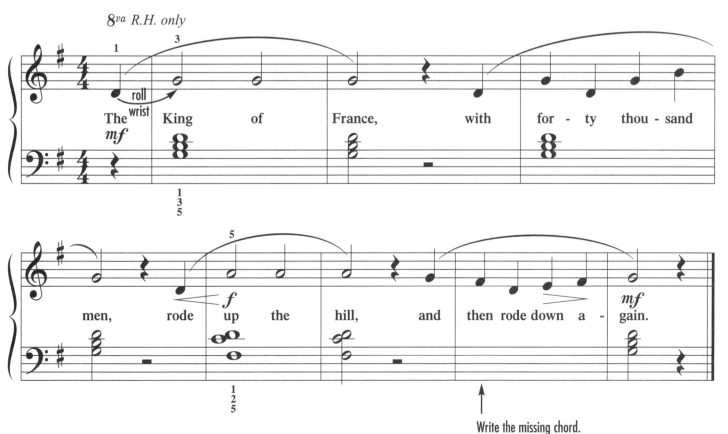

8va R.H. only

The King of France, with for-ty thou-sand

mf roll wrist

men, rode up the hill, and then rode down a-gain.

f *mf*

Write the missing chord.

Rhythm Review

1. Add bar lines to each rhythm pattern below. Then clap and count aloud, whispering the rests.

Tempo Review

2. Draw a line from each composer to the tempo that matches below. Then write in the counting to each pattern and tap and count aloud with the metronome.

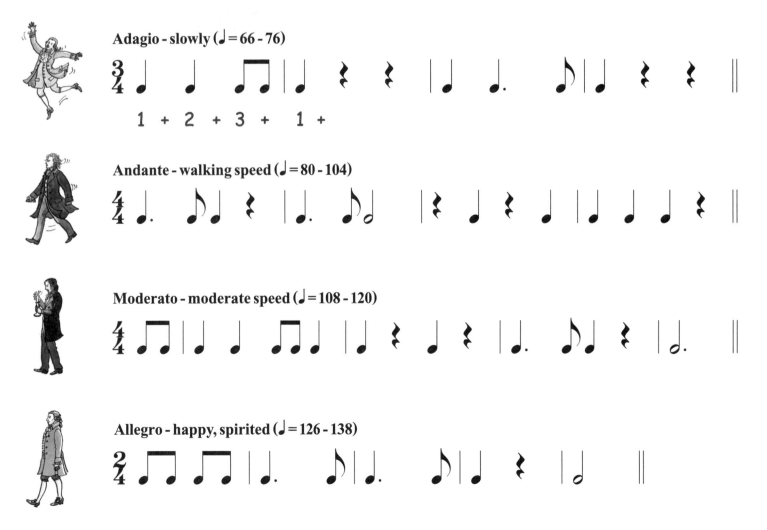

Adagio - slowly ($\quad$ = 66 - 76)

1 + 2 + 3 + 1 +

Andante - walking speed ($\quad$ = 80 - 104)

Moderato - moderate speed ($\quad$ = 108 - 120)

Allegro - happy, spirited ($\quad$ = 126 - 138)

Parrot Play:

- Your teacher will play *Clementine.*
- Sing it together. Circle the only 6th.
- By ear, play each phrase after your teacher plays it.

Clementine

In a cav - ern, in a can - yon, ex - ca - va - ting for a mine, lived a

Oh my dar - ling, oh my dar - ling, oh my dar - ling, Clem-en - tine, you are

mi - er for - ty nin - er, and his daugh - ter, Clem - en - tine.

lost and gone for - ev - er, dread - ful sor - ry, Clem - en - tine.

(For teachers: After students can play *Clementine,* you may wish to experiment with rhythm or note changes to see if your students hear the mistake(s).)

Time to Compose:

- Make up your own ending to *The More We Get Together* (p. 20 Lesson Book).
- Play the piece to the downbeat of measure 16 and then write a new ending below! Be sure to end on the tonic.

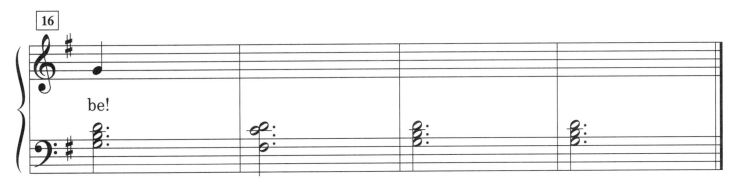

be!

The D Major Scale

- In the D Major scale below, write the letter names above each note. Then mark the two half steps.

- Notice that the key of D Major needs two sharps (F♯ and C♯) to keep the major pattern.

Key signature

- Now write "I" below the tonic notes, "V" below the dominant note, and "LT" under the leading tone. Play these notes on the piano.

- Trace the F♯ and C♯ in the key signature below.

- Then draw the key signature for D Major twice on your own.

 • Play the **last sharp** in the key signature and go **up** a half step. You are on D. That is the name of the key—D Major.

- Write a D Major scale in the Treble Clef, ascending and descending. Keep in mind to write the ♯'s in front of the correct notes.

- Draw the key signature for D Major.
- Then write a D Major scale, ascending and descending.

Visiting Grasslands

- There are many animals that make grasslands their home.
- Complete each musical example as you take the path from one animal to the next one.

1. **A skillful coyote:**
- Complete the D Major cadence in the R.H. Circle the leading tone.
- Add the fingering.

2. **Protective wolves:**
- Complete the D Major cadence in the L.H. Circle the leading tone.
- Add the fingering.

3. **A flock of geese:**
- Write the correct fingering for an **ascending** D Major scale in the L.H.

4. **A cool and calm bobcat:**
- Write the correct fingering for a **descending** D Major scale in the R.H.

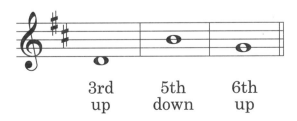

5. **Majestic bison:**
- Write the following harmonic intervals in D Major:

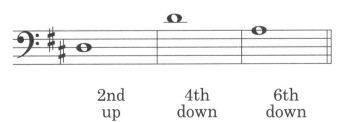

6. **Wild turkeys:**
- Write the following melodic intervals in D Major:

3rd up	5th down	6th up

2nd up	4th down	6th down

At the Baseball Diamond

- Circle the correct answer in each pair for a home run!

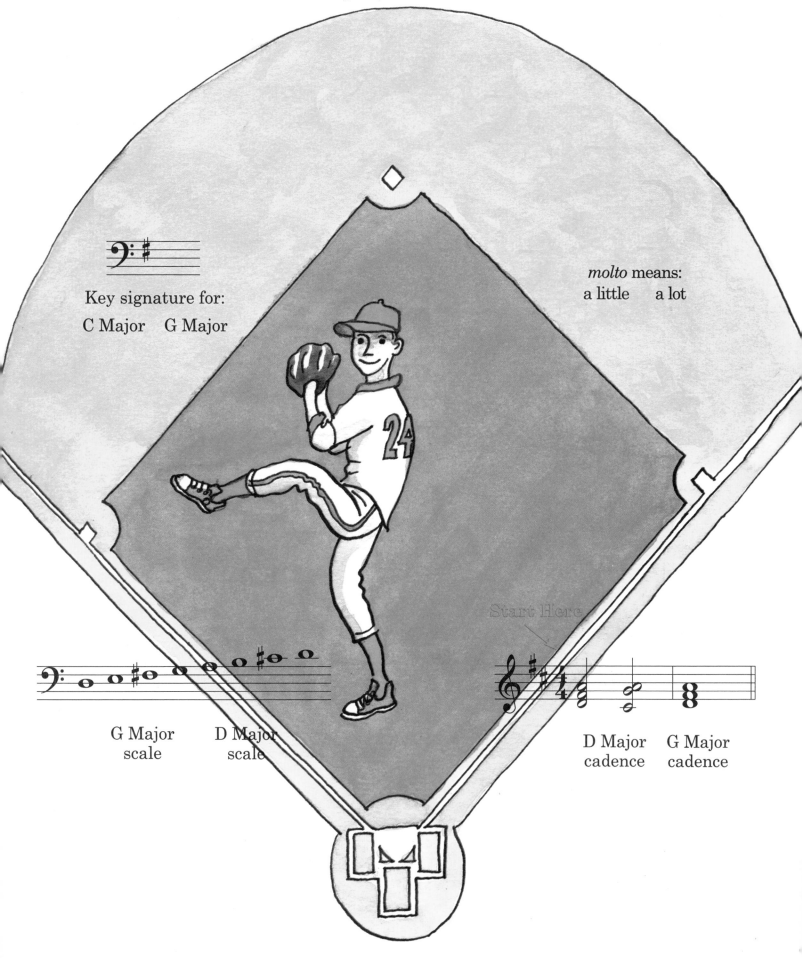

Key signature for:

C Major   G Major

molto means:
a little   a lot

G Major
scale

D Major
scale

D Major
cadence

G Major
cadence

Follow the Leader:

- Look at the music on the right.
- Listen to your teacher clap a rhythm.
- Can you clap it back?
- Circle the one you hear, a or b.

Ear Training:

- Your teacher will play tonic (I) and dominant (V^7) chords.
- Which one do you hear first? Which one do you hear second?
- Write I and V^7 in the correct order on each line.

1. _____   2. _____   3. _____

For teacher use:

To be played in any order.   To be played in any order.

Review of Intervals and Note Names

- Name each interval (except repeated notes).
- Then play the piece, naming the intervals.
- Play the piece again, saying the letter name of the notes.

Old Brass Wagon
American

Cir-cle to the left, old brass wag-on, cir-cle to the left, old brass wag-on.

Cir-cle to the left, old brass wag-on; you're the one, my dar-lin'.

- Transpose to D Major.

Eggs and Toast — Ledger Line Notes

- Play each interval on the left.
- Draw a line from each interval on an egg to its match in the correct piece of toast. **Ex.**

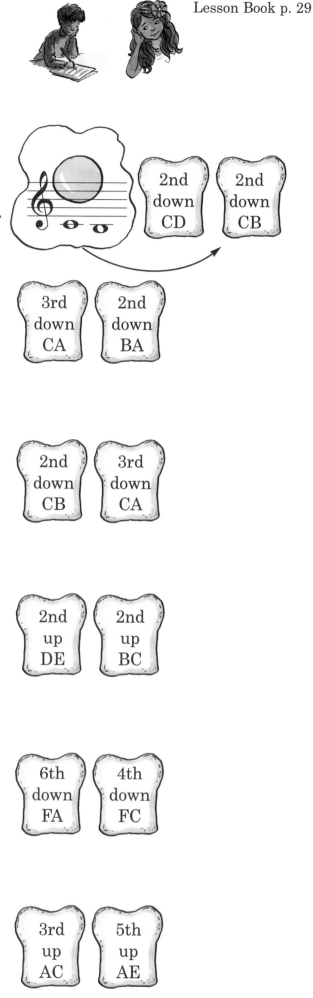

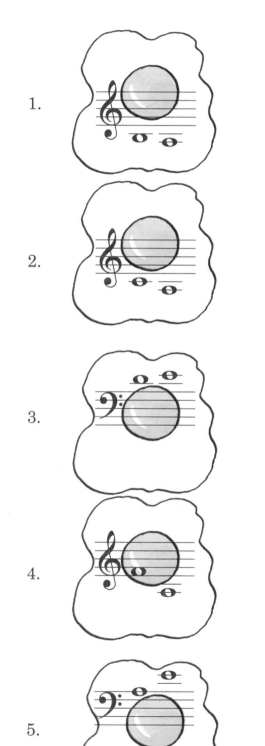

1.

2.

3.

4.

5.

FJH2068

Ledger Line Notes above the Treble Staff

FACE

• Name the following intervals and notes.

Ex. **3rd up** _____ _____ _____ _____ _____ _____

F   A

_____ _____ _____ _____ _____ _____

_____ _____ _____ _____ _____ _____

• Circle the correct note in each tree trunk.

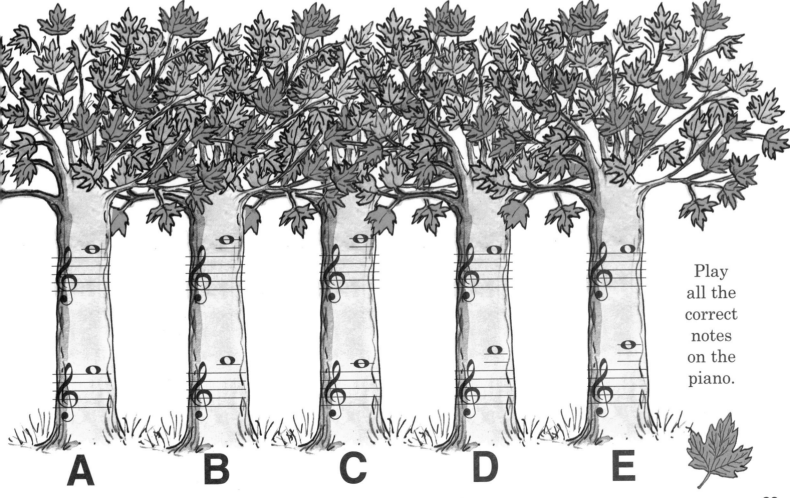

A **B** **C** **D** **E**

Play all the correct notes on the piano.

Help The Tuba Player Find His Notes!

- The tuba player forgot his glasses and can't see his music.
- Name the following numbered intervals and notes.

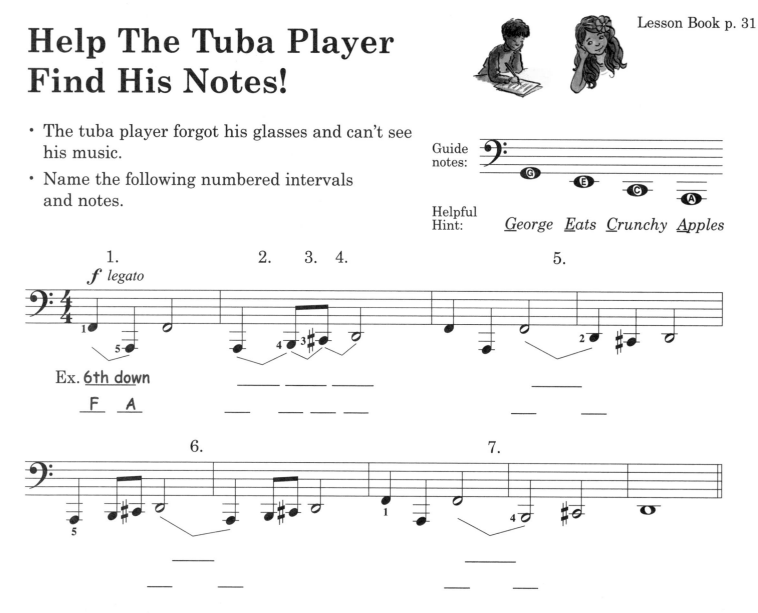

Guide notes:

Helpful Hint: *George* *Eats* *Crunchy* *Apples*

- Now play the piece on the piano.

Another Helpful Hint:

All *Cows* *Eat* *Grass*

FJH2068

Follow the Leader:

- Listen to your teacher clap a rhythm. Do you hear a or b?
- Can you clap it back?

a.

b.

Time to Compose:

- Using one of the rhythms on the left, make up your own piece in AB or ABA form. Use ledger line notes.

Possible titles: *Tightrope Walker, In a Cave.*

My title: _____

Head and Shoulders, Knees and Toes

- Add the time signature below.
- Add in the counting. The first measure has been done for you.
- Step the ♩ beats while clapping the rhythm of the song.
- Then, can you say the words and do the motions?

1 + 2 + 3 + 4 +
Head and shoul-ders, knees and toes, knees and toes!

Head and shoul-ders, knees and toes, knees and toes,

eyes and ears and mouth and cheeks and nose,

head and shoul-ders, knees and toes, knees and toes!

The A Major Scale

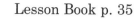

- Write the A Major scale below.
- Then mark the two half steps.
- Notice that the key of A Major needs three sharps (F♯, C♯, and G♯) to keep the major pattern.

Key signature

- Trace the sharps in the key signature below.
- Then draw the key signature for A Major twice on your own.

- Play the **last sharp** in the key signature and go **up** a half step.
  You are on A. That is the name of the key—A Major.

- Draw the key signature for A Major.
- Then write an A Major scale, ascending and descending.

FJH2068

Going On Safari

- As you meet the animals on the safari, complete the musical examples.

1. **Wise elephants:**

- Complete the A Major cadence in the L.H.

- Add the fingering.

2. **At the lion's lair:**

- Complete the A Major cadence in the R.H.

- Add the fingering.

3. **A troop of monkeys:**

- Circle the correct fingering for an **ascending** A Major scale in the R.H.

1 2 3 1 2 3 4 5
1 2 3 4 1 2 3 4

4. **Digging warthogs:**

- Write the correct fingering for a **descending** A Major scale in the L.H.

5. **The tiger's trail:**

- Write the following harmonic intervals in A Major.

5th up   4th down   6th up

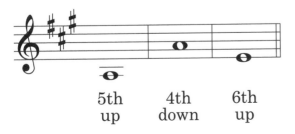

6. **Playful rhinoceros:**

- Write the following melodic intervals in A Major.

3rd down   2nd up   6th down

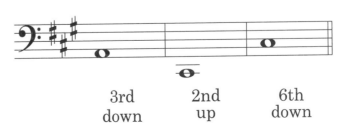

Follow the Leader:

- Listen to your teacher clap a rhythm.
- Then clap it back.

For teacher use:
(Use any of these rhythms or others you might like!)

(Students will learn triplets in Grade 3A!)

Parrot Play:

- Your teacher will play an A Major scale.
- Then your teacher will play one example from each set below.
- Can you play it back? (Watch and listen carefully!)
- Circle the one you hear.

Ear Training:

- Your teacher will play some intervals. Listen carefully!
- Write 2nd, 3rd, 4th, 5th, or 6th.

1. _____ 2. _____ 3. _____

4. _____ 5. _____

For teacher use: (To be played in any order.)

FJH2068

UNIT 8

At The Concert Hall

Win as many orchestra tickets as you can so you can take your family and friends to hear a concert of beautiful music.

- Complete each minor five-finger pattern and cadence below by filling in the missing notes. Add sharps and flats if needed.

- Your teacher will check your answers and write in the total number of tickets. (You win 2 tickets for every correct example.)

Ear Training:

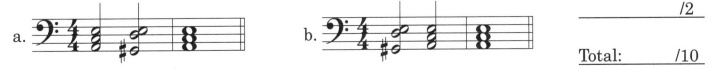

Extra tickets are still available!

- Your teacher will play two minor cadences. **One** will be i-V⁷-i.

- Without looking at the piano, name the correct cadence, a or b.

Legato Pedaling.

- Use the damper pedal to connect notes or chords without a break in sound.

- This pedal also makes the playing sound fuller and richer because the piano strings vibrate freely.

Time to Compose:

- Finish the piece below.
- Draw the pedal markings for the last two measures.
- Then play it.

Faraway Place

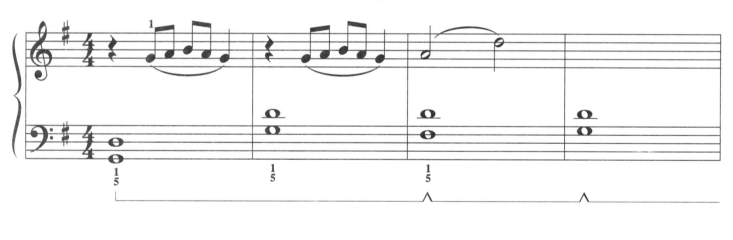

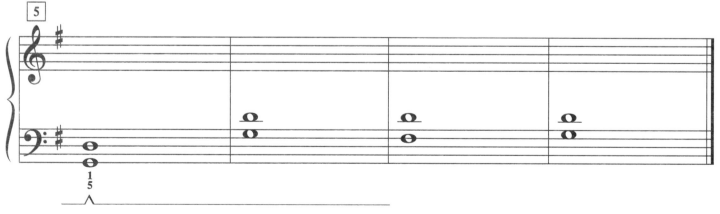

FJH2068

Ear Training:

- Listen to your teacher play two scales.

- Which scale sounds major? Which sounds minor?
  Tell your teacher after (s)he plays both of them.

  For teacher use: (To be played in any order.)

(Major)   (minor)

  Play any other major and minor scales and see how well your students hear the difference!
  (Or, play major and minor hand over hand arpeggios!)

Time to Compose:

- Play the A section of *Russian Dance* below.

- Create a B section using the same L.H. harmony as the A section.

Russian Dance

- How would you make this piece ABA form?
  Circle one: add a *D.C. al Fine*   play the B section again.

As Fast as a High-Speed Train

(Review of Major and Minor)

- Use a clock and time yourself.
- Write in the answers to the 12 examples below.

- Draw the following:

Major 3rd up: 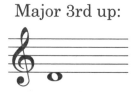   Minor 3rd up:    Major 3rd up:    Minor 3rd up:

Minor 3rd up:    Major 3rd up: Minor 3rd up:    Major 3rd up:

- Circle the following:

Minor cadence:    Major cadence:

Minor cadence:    Major cadence:

- Now play **all** the examples on the page.

Your time to complete the entire page: _____ minutes _____ seconds

The Eighth Rest

♪   Eighth note = 1/2 beat

𝄾   Eighth rest = 1/2 beat of silence

• Trace these eighth rests: 𝄾 𝄾 𝄾 𝄾

Draw 2 eighth rests on your own:

The Wise Old Owl

• Write in the counting below.
• Choose one note on the piano, and play this piece, counting aloud.
• Then tap each ♩ pulse with your foot while saying the words.

```
+    1 + 2 + 3 + 4 +    1 + 2 + 3 + 4 +
A   wise old owl    sat  in an oak;   The more  he heard,   the
```

```
less   he   spoke.   The   less   he   spoke,   the   more   he   heard;
```

```
Why aren't we all   like that   wise   old   bird?
```

Rhythm Review

- Circle the measures that have too few beats.
- Fix them by adding rests and then clap and count aloud.

Rain, Rain, Everywhere!

- Draw a line from each dynamic level to the picture it matches.

pp p mp mf f ff

FJH2068

UNIT 9

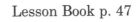

The F Major Scale

- Write the F Major scale below.
- Then mark the two half steps.
- Notice that the key of F Major needs one flat (B♭) to keep the major pattern.

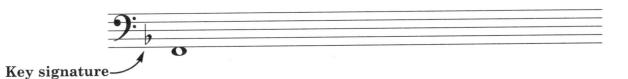

Key signature

- Now, write "I" below the tonic notes, "V" below the dominant note, and "LT" under the leading tone. Play these notes on the piano.

- Trace the B♭ in the key signature below.
- Then draw the key signature for F Major twice on your own.

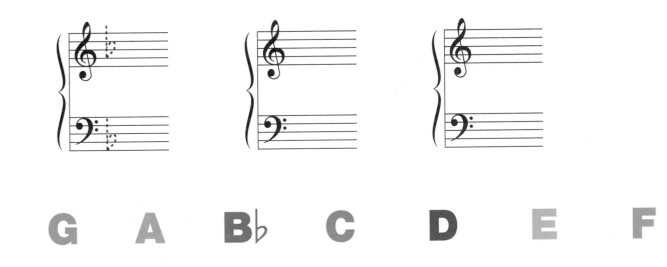

F   G   A   B♭   C   D   E   F

- Draw the key signature for F Major..
- Then write an F Major scale, ascending and descending.

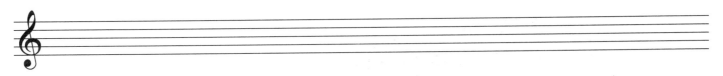

- Can you **close your eyes** and say the letter names of the F Major scale? Memorize it today!

FJH2068

You're Going Places!

- Correct the mistake in each kind of transportation.
- Then play each musical example.

I

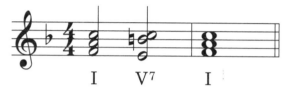

I   V⁷   I

I   V⁷   I

FJH2068

It's Matching Time

Draw a line for each key signature on the left to the
correct answer on the right.

Key of:

C Major

G Major

D Major

A Major

F Major

Time to Compose:

- Make up your own variation on *Twinkle, Twinkle Little Star.*
- Circle at least **three** terms in the following list you will use.

melody in R.H.	I-V⁷-I chords	*pp*
melody in L.H.	broken triad bass	*ff*
harmonic 3rds	waltz bass	𝄽
finger crossings	damper pedal	

★ Practice your piece as many
times as it takes to completely
remember it! Play it after you
play the other 2 variations of
Twinkle, Twinkle Little Star
in your Lesson Book.

Ear Training:

- Circle the 6ths in *Goodbye, Old Paint*.
- Play the melody.
- Then block the L.H. accompaniment.
  The three V⁷ chords are marked for you. Use the I triad for all of the other measures.

Goodbye, Old Paint

American Cowboy Song

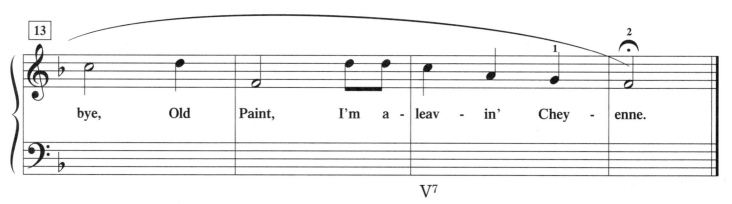

☐ Check the box when you can play this song.　☐ Experiment with a broken triad bass or
　　　　　　　　　　　　　　　　　　　　　　　a waltz bass.

- Your teacher might wish to experiment with a note or rhythm change to see if you can hear it. Good luck!

Hall of Fame—
Know the Composers

- You have met quite a few composers along your way to learning how to play.
  Rewrite their names on the lines. Can you say their names?

- The three composers at the bottom are new for this grade.

- Choose one **new** composer and tell your teacher something about him.

**Franz Joseph
"Papa" Haydn**

Mozart

Beethoven

Chopin

Schumann

Bizet

Brahms

Vivaldi

New composers:

Borodin

Copland

Saint-Saëns

(Lesson Book p. 29)   (Lesson Book p. 10-11)   (Recital Book p. 16-17)

Certificate of Achievement

_____

Student

has completed

Helen Marlais'
Succeeding at the Piano®

Theory and Activity Book

GRADE 2B

You are now ready for

GRADE 3A

_____   _____

Date   Teacher's Signature

T H E
F·J·H
MUSIC
COMPANY
I N C.
Frank J. Hackinson